CW00722247

CHARACTERS

RUBY

GRIFF

NURSE

THE PLAY TAKES PLACE IN A CORRIDOR OUTSIDE A SMALL HOSPITAL ROOM.

OUTSIDE THIS ROOM IS A DOOR AND PART OF A WALL. AGAINST THIS WALL ARE TWO CHAIRS. RUBY, A WOMAN IN HER MID FIFTIES IS SITTING IN ONE OF THEM. SHE IS WEARING THE UNIFORM OF A LOLLI-POP LADY. HER HAT IS ON THE CHAIR NEXT TO HER. SHE HAS A SHOPPING BAG ON HER LAP AND A LARGE WHITE MANS HANKY IN HER HAND. SHE IS WIPING HER NOSE AS THE LIGHTS COME UP - WE KNOW INSTANTLY THOUGH THAT SHE IS NOT DOING THIS BECAUSE SHE HAS A COLD.

JANGLING INSTRUMENT NOISES.

A MALE NURSE COMES OUT OF THE ROOM CARRYING A TRAY COVERED BY A WHITE CLOTH.

NURSE: Back in a minute.

RUBY: Is that it? Can I go in now, nurse?

NURSE: SHAKING HIS HEAD. Not quite finished with him yet. Shouldn't be long though.

RUBY: How is he this morning?

NURSE: A definite improvement on yesterday I'd say.

PAUSING SLIGHTLY BEFORE MAKING TO LEAVE S.R.

RUBY: I heard somebody laughing just now. Was it him?

NURSE: No, it was me. He's a real live wire once he starts, isn't he?

RUBY: He's hell of a boy mind. He's never happy unless he's making people laugh..

RUBY LAUGHS AND SO DOES THE NURSE.

NURSE: Ten minutes and he should be ready for an audience.

RUBY: Good God he's told you as well as he?

NURSE: Sorry?

RUBY: That's the best way to be though I suppose. I keep telling Griff, that's my husband, things will be much better now it's all out in the open, I said. He's only just recently found out. I've known for a while. It's not so bad when you've had time to get use to the idea.

THE NURSE SUDDENLY REALISES WHAT RUBY IS ON ABOUT. HE SMILES BEFORE LEAVING.

NURSE: Be back in a minute.

AFTER A SECOND OR TWO RUBY GETS UP AND LOOKS INTO THE ROOM THROUGH THE ROUND HOLE IN THE DOOR. SHE CAN'T REALLY SEE ANYTHING SO SHE SITS BACK DOWN. SHE DRIES HER NOSE AGAIN. GRIFF WALKS ON FROM S.L. HE IS ABOUT THE SAME AGE AS RUBY. HE IS WEARING HIS GUARDS UNIFORM COMPLETE WITH HAT. RUBY LOOKS UP AND SEES HIM.

RUBY: WIPING HER EYES NOW. Griff. You came after all.

GRIFF: Let's get this straight now before we start, right? I'm not here for him it's you I've come for.

RUBY: Shshsh .... You can't say that, he's our son.

GRIFF: He might be your son, Ruby, but I told him Saturday night, if he was going to carry on with all that nonsense he'd be no son of mine. I meant it then, and accident or no I mean it now.

RUBY: RAISING HER VOICE. Don't talk like that - he might never come out of there.

GRIFF: SHOUTING BACK. He's got a couple of bruises, a few fractured ribs and he's had a knock on the head. He's not going to die, Ruby. He'll be out of this place by Thursday - you take it from me.

RUBY: Look here, he didn't come round hardly at all yesterday. He talked nonsense for a solid hour last night.

GRIFF: He's been talking nonsense since last Saturday if you ask me.

RUBY: Well I'm not asking you - and I told you this morning, you've got to forget last Saturday -

GRIFF: I can't.

RUBY: Well you're going to have to. For the moment, anyway.

GRIFF: It's like a bloody nightmare. It keeps playing over and over in my head.

RUBY: There's no way he'll be out of here this weekend. He's in no fit state.
            SHE HAS A THOUGHT. They're hiding something from me I'm sure of it.

GRIFF: Don't talk rubbish.

RUBY: They are, I can tell.

GRIFF: They've said he's all right.

RUBY: Yes but they're not going to tell me everything, are they? And you must
            be concerned as well if the truth be known because nothing couldn't shift
            you to come here with me this morning. SHE HAS AN IDEA. They
            haven't sent for you have they?

GRIFF: No.

RUBY: They haven't rung you from the hospital to come here, have they?

GRIFF: Would I be dressed for the afternoon shift if there was anything wrong?

RUBY: Tell me why you changed your mind, then?

GRIFF: For you. I changed it for you. I didn't want you to be on your own.

A SLIGHT PAUSE.

GRIFF SITS DOWN AND TAKES A PACK OF SANDWICHES OUT OF HIS BAG.

RUDY: A LOUD WHISPER. There was a policeman here earlier on.. He
            confirmed there was no other car involved.

GRIFF: So what do they think happened then?

RUBY: They know what happened. He fell asleep at the wheel.

GRIFF: Well I'm not-surprised - should never be doing two jobs. I don lt know
            anyone who can survive on three or four hours sleep.

RUBY: Yes, he's been over doing it lately.

GRIFF: Sandwich?

RUBY: Good God no, I can't eat.

GRIFF: PAUSE. When he gets out later this week - perhaps you'd better suggest him giving up that "club" lark.

RUBY: I'm not suggesting anything of the sort.

GRIFF: Well he's hardly going to listen to me, is he?

RUBY: You still don't get it do you, Griff? If Nigel decides, for whatever reason, to give up one of his jobs, it'll be his day job in ~~Cardiff~~. It's not going to be the clubs Griff, you can put money on that. _GLASGOW_

GRIFF: Lets be honest, you wouldn't talk him out of doing it anyway, even if he would listen to you.

RUBY: No you're right, I wouldn't.

GRIFF: God, you must be as proud as he is.

RUBY: I am. He's damned good at what he does and you thought so too before you realised who it was.

GRIFF: A PAUSE. HE LOOKS AT HER. I'll never forgive him for that - or you either

RUBY: How else was the boy supposed to tell you.

GRIFF: Like any other normal person.

RUBY: Griff, if he was normal he'd have had nothing to say.

GRIFF: Am I that bad a father that I couldn't be told in the privacy of my own house?

RUBY: In a word, yes. SHE HELPS HERSELF TO A SANDWICH. You know what you were like when he wouldn't take that job with you on the railway.

GRIFF: That was a damn good job.

RUBY: But he didn't want it.

GRIFF: _GLASGOW_

No - he,d rather go and dress windows in ~~Cardiff~~. The writing was on the wall even then. SLIGHT PAUSE. Well that's it as far as the club is concerned, you know that don't you?

RUBY: What do you mean?

GRIFF: We're in every Saturday night from now on because there's no way I can show my face in that place again.

RUBY: Oh for goodness sake - anyone would think he robbed a bank or murdered somebody or something.

GRIFF: I think I could cope better with it if he had.

RUBY: Look, it's not easy for me either mind.

GRIFF: I was the butt of all the jokes in work yesterday.

RUBY: Well that's just great that is, isn't it? There they all were in the club Saturday night -

GRIFF: Exactly -

RUBY: All your workmates having a marvellous time, and today? Today they mock him for it.

GRIFF: It's not Nigel they were mocking - it was me.

RUBY: You think you're by yourself in that? I get it. I get it in supermarkets and in bus queues..... I get it when I stop them in their cars to let the children cross the road. It happened last week. The car window was rolled down and I actually this woman say. "See her by there? Her son dresses up in women's clothes", I waited til the last kid was across the road then I stood right in front of her car. "My son is a female impersonator", I said. "He does it f or a living. I heard your husband does it for kicks. With that, the car revved up and I swear to God, if I hadn't stepped out of the way when I did I think she'd have run me over.

PAUSE.

GRIFF: It sounds like everyone knew except me. PAUSE.

RUBY: He tried to tell you...

GRIFF: So when did you find out?

RUBY: Well, I as down his house and I went in the bedroom dusting and saw he'd left the wardrobe door open. There were all these beautiful dresses in there. So I asked him about it and he told me.

GRIFF: He'd have told you eventually anyway. You've always been close, and that's half the trouble. SHE LOOKS AT HIM. Don't look at me like that, it's true. SLIGHT PAUSE. Me and him... we've never had anything going for us. He's embarrassed me all my life.

RUBY: The trouble with you is you've got a short memory. You want to think back to Saturday night in the club.

GRIFF: I don't have to think back to it - I can't get the bloody thing out of my brain.

RUBY: You were having a marvellous time.

GRIFF: And that's what hurts the most.

RUBY: Tell me why you like drag acts, Griff? (KNOWS)

GRIFF: I don't know.... they're a bit of fun, I suppose.

RUBY: Exactly. You thought "The Dolly Sisters" were the best act the club had booked in months. You were killing yourself laughing, I know because I watched you. You laughed so much I thought you weren't going to stop.

GRIFF: And the fact is I haven't laughed once since.

RUBY: They were marvellous. Nigel and his friend.... Everybody loved them, they were so professional. All right, maybe it was cruel to call you up on the stage with them but you were glad to go at the time. You were having a ball. SLIGHT PAUSE. Until Nigel took his wig off.

GRIFF: I wanted to die.

RUBY: I swear to God I didn't know he was going to do that. And in fairness I don't think he'd planned it either. I think he just siezed the moment when he could.

GRIFF: QUIETLY. I just wanted to crawl in a corner and die.

RUBY: You hid your feelings pretty well then.

GRIFF: No I didn't. PAUSE. When I wiped my eyes everyone thought, including you, it was because I was laughing so much and it was... until I realised it was my boy up there. SLIGHT PAUSE. You can't imagine how I felt.

RUBY: Of course I can.

GRIFF: No you can't. It's different for a father.

RUBY: In what way?

GRIFF: I can't explain it.

RUBY: Try.

GRIFF: I felt so -

RUBY: Disappointed?

GRIFF: HE TRIES TO FIND THE WORDS. Cheated.

RUBY: Even after all the laughter.

GRIFF: Because of all the laughter.

RUBY: You're saying you'd have taken it better if they didn't like him so much.

GRIFF: It would have been a lot less embarrassing for me, yes.

RUBY: So you'd rather he had died up on that stage?

GRIFF: QUIETLY. Yes.

RUBY: Is that what you're saying?

GRIFF: SHOUTING. Yes!

RUBY: SLIGHT PAUSE. Nigel didn't do anything that you haven't done in the past.

GRIFF: What are you talking about?

RUBY: You've dressed up as a woman before now.

GRIFF: I have not!

RUBY: What about that Blackpool trip we went on?

GRIFF: That was a long time ago.

RUBY: I can remember you prancing up and down the aisle wearing my green lurex dress and Mary Morgan's hair piece - and I'm sure Nigel can. There's a photo of you too, somewhere.

GRIFF: That was only a bit of fun.

RUBY: And last Saturday night wasn't?

GRIFF: That's a different thing altogether.

RUBY: But it's not..... not really. The only difference is that you entertained 40 people on a bus and he entertained four hundred in a club.

GRIFF: No, no.... now you can say what you like, there' a lot more to it than that.

RUBY: Tell me why you did it, Griff?

GRIFF: SLIGHT PAUSE. I don't know.... I was probably drunk.

RUBY: Come on .... you can do better than that.

GRIFF: I can't remember.

RUBY: I can.

GRIFF: Then what do you want me to tell you for?

RUBY: I want to hear you say it. SLIGHT PAUSE. O.K. I'll help you out. You always saw yourself as a bit of a lad, didn't you? Hard to imagine looking at you now, but you still like attention, Griff - Nigel follows you for that. That's why you were quite happy to join the drag queens up on the stage. You like making people laugh. The trouble is you think that last Saturday the joke was on you.

GRIFF: It was.

RUBY: Then it was on me too.

GRIFF: No it wasn't. You knew who you were looking at. You knew why you were laughing.

RUBY: I wasn't laughing at you Griff, and neither was anyone else.

GRIFF: They might not have laughed at me at the time but they've laughed at me enough since.I'm the talk of the place. We all are. SLIGHT PAUSE. I shouldn't have found out the way I did.

RUBY: No, I know, love. Only last week I said to him "You'd better tell your father quick", I said. "You take that booking at the club and sooner or later he's bound to find out". SLIGHT PAUSE. I think the plan was to tell you after his spot - or later when we got home but you were enjoying the show so much...

GRIFF: SLIGHT PAUSE Do you think he's... ? He isn't is he... ?

RUBY: What?

GRIFF: You know what I mean.

THEY LOOK AT EACH OTHER FOR A BRIEF MOMENT.

RUBY: They say it doesn't go hand in hand but...... yes. SLIGHT PAUSE. Do you know what hurts me the most. Not that he'll never get married... but that I'll never show a little grandchild over the crossing and in to school. SLIGHT PAUSE. And then I thought, well there's nothing I can do about it, you can't have the penny and the bun. I'm going to have to settle for the fact that my son is a cabaret artist and a very good one at that.

GRIFF: I wish it was that easy for me.

RUBY: It's not a question of it being easy, Griff. Our hands are tied. We play the game with the cards we're dealt. We either accept him for what he is or we don't. SLIGHT PAUSE. Do you know how he told me? GRIFF SHAKES HIS HEAD. Do you want to know? HE NODS. I suppose it was about two years ago now. It was a Saturday morning and you were in work. I knew there was something up, he was hanging around my feet, you know generally getting in the way. In the end I said, "Come on, what is it? You've obviously got something on your mind so spit it out". He was at the table and he told me to sit down. I did and the atmosphere changed. The sparkle went from his eyes and he came over all serious. I didn't like it at all. "What is it" I said, "you're frightening me". He held his arms out across the table and grabbed me by the hands so tight I could see the whites of his knuckles. He looked me straight in the eye. "I've got a brain tumour" he said, "and I've only got three months to live". oh my God, I could feel myself floating off. Then he yanked my hands and it suddenly brought me back. "No I haven't", he said. "It's all right, I'm not going to die. I'm only gay". I could have killed him... but I kissed him instead.

A PAUSE. AT THIS POINT THE NURSE RETURNS.

NURSE: ON SEEING GRIFF Oh, Mister Gregory. Nigel asked me if you were here. I'll tell him.

GRIFF: Er, no..... SLIGHT PAUSE. I'm not staying.

NURSE: Oh... can't you pop your head round? I'm not going to be very much longer.

GRIFF: I've got to get to work.

NURSE: All right - go on - nip in now then. You've got time to show your face.

GRIFF: SHOUTING. No I said! You bloody deaf or what?

NURSE LOOKS AT RUBY BEFORE GOING IN TO NIGEL.

RUBY: You're going to be a very lonely old man, Griff.

GRIFF: You never tried, not once.... not once when he was growing up to interest him in...

RUBY: Hey, you can't blame me. Now it's not my fault. That's the first thing Nigel said to me. He said, "Now look Mam", he said, "You mustn't blame yourself ", and I don't. How he's turned out has got nothing to do with me at all.

GRIFF: You saying it's my fault?

RUBY: You're the one who dressed up and entertained the bus from Blackpool. Who's to say what put the idea into his head.

GRIFF: You don't think it was that, do you?

RUBY: SLIGHT PAUSE No, Griff . You didn't make him what he is and neither did I.

GRIFF: We must have done something.

RUBY: All I've done is to accept him for what he is because he's my son and because I love him.

GRIFF: I can't think like that.

RUBY: You still love him, don't you? HE DOESN'T ANSWER. If you don't feel the same as me then I feel sorry because you're going to miss out. You're going to miss out on something very special.

GRIFF: Special?

RUBY: SLIGHT PAUSE. You're a hypocrite Griffith Gregory, and not a very nice one at that.

GRIFF: Is there any other kind?

RUBY: A THOUGHT STRIKES HER. It's Monday. Did you remember to put the rubbish out before you came?

GRIFF: Have I ever forgot?

RUBY: SLIGHT PAUSE. Everything will be all right in the end. HE LOOKS AT HER. We've still got him that's all that matters. We could have lost him in that car crash. How would you have felt then?

GRIFF: A lot like I do now, I suppose. I've lost him anyway.

RUBY: Look, when you go in there and you see him

GRIFF: I'm not going in there. I told you when I came here it was only for you.

RUBY: I'm sure he wants to see you.

GRIFF: Well we can't all have what we want.

RUBY: Refusing to see or speak to him isn't going to make it better.

GRIFF: And going in there is?

RUBY: It's not going to make it any worse.

GRIFF: I can't go in there. I can't look him in the face.

RUBY: Why, it's the same face you looked at last week.

GRIFF: It's the same face I looked at last Saturday... minus the make-up.

RUBY: And wig. Don't forget the wig.

GRIFF: It's not funny.

RUBY: Of course it is.... it's bloody hysterical. We' ll all be laughing about it in a couple of months time.

GRIFF: I should have put my foot down.

RUBY: What?

GRIFF: I saw it coming. I knew the way things were going right from early on. SLIGHT PAUSE. I should have done something.... took him to football matches and -

RUBY: Oh for goodness sake, what's matter with you. You don't honestly think watching twenty-two men kicking a ball around would have made any difference? You don't live in the real world, you don't. Buying him a cowby outfit for Christmas when he was small instead of a Post Office set wouldn't have changed anything - even I know that. SLIGHT PAUSE. You' re doing what I first did, you're blaming yourself and you shouldn't. You're looking for a reason and there isn't one.

GRIFF: There's got to be.

RUBY: Look, I am what I am, you are what you are and he is what he is. At the end of the day thank God we're not all the same.

GRIFF: DURING THIS SPEECH GRIFF RUNS AWAY WITH HIMSELF. What went wrong then? Tell me I need to know because something somewhere went wrong. There must have been a time when he realised he was what he was. I mean you don't just wake up one day and choose to be something like that, and if it's got nothing to do with you or me and the way he was brought up then what has it got to do with? Where's the reasons for it? I don't believe it when you say there isn't one. Why didn't he tell us about it at the time, maybe he could have had help, we could have taken him to see somebody who could have talked to him, who could have listened to him and then all this could have been avoided. A THOUGHT HITS HIM. Maybe it' s not too late? He could go private - we can pay. I bet it would only take a few sessions with someone who knew what they were doing, someone recommended who could get to the heart of his trouble straight away. I don't think it's as big a problem as it first looks, it's only a question of preference, isn't it? So it couldn't be difficult to find someone who could straighten him out. Get him to see it's only a matter of choice and once all that's sorted, I'm sure the other thing the dressing up thing will right itself. What do you think?

RUBY: SLIGHT PAUSE. Look Griff.... I don't know much about it - I suppose there are books you can get on it but I'm sure as hell not going in to the library to ask for one. All I know are the few bits and pieces Nigel has told me. From what I can gather it's not a life threatening disease, apart from this aids thing, and it's not something you can go and have "straightened out" either. It's not like having a tooth pulled and then that's it it's gone - everything's back to normal. SLIGHT PAUSE. If it's only a matter of preference like you say, is it really that big a deal he prefers something else? I know it's disappointing and I know it's not what we want..... but we don It have a choice... and although you'll find this hard to believe, I don't think Nigel had much of a say in it either. You don't choose to be different.... you just are.

GRIFF: I can't understand how it's all so "matter of fact", with you.

RUBY: Oh don't think he didn't break my heart because he did. I've lost count how many nights I cried myself to sleep. And what made it harder for me was I couldn't show him or you. I had to cry on my own and carry on as if nothing had happened even though my world was collapsing around me. SLIGHT PAUSE. "I'm glad I told you" he said. "It's like taking a big weight off my chest." Trouble was he took it off his chest and put it on mine. I'm not complaining. That's what mothers are for. SLIGHT PAUSE. Do you know what did help me though? HE DOESN'T ANSWER. I picked up my magazine one week and some mother had written in to say that her son was going through the same thing, and do you know what the advice was? HE STILL DOESN'T ANSWER. I can't remember it now word for word but it was something like.... There are two things parents should give their children, it said. Roots and wings. Roots and wings, Griff. Our Nigel knows there's always a room for him at home and -

GRIFF: Does that mean he's coming to us when he gets out of here?

RUBY: I don't know. I haven't talked to him about it yet but I hope so. SLIGHT PAUSE. Whatever he wants to do, Griff or wherever he wants to fly... it's okay with me. I'm behind him all the way. All I want is for him to be happy and there's nothing I wouldn't do to make sure he is.

GRIFF: What if I said he can't come home?

RUBY: What if I said you can bugger off?

GRIFF: He's left home - it's not fair to encourage him back.

RUBY: What's fair got to do with it? He'll need to recuperate. Kevin will do his best I'm sure.

GRIFF: Who the hell is Kevin?

RUBY: Nigel's friend. The other half of the act.

GRIFF: SLIGHT PAUSE Wait a minute. You're not going to tell met that they live together, are you?

RUBY: Well I was going to but it's pointless now.

GRIFF: I don't believe this.

RUBY: You're going to have to learn to be more tolerant, Griff. Shouldn't be difficult - you've always said, "Live and let live".

GRIFF: Yes but not when it's your own flesh and blood.

RUBY: It should apply even more then.

GRIFF: So my son lives with another man. Is there anything else I should know?

RUBY: No I think that's everything.

GRIFF: You sure? You're not keeping anything back to protect me from having a heart attack, are you?

RUBY: There's the little one they're expecting in June, but apart from that there's nothing.

GRIFF: I wish I could joke about it.

RUBY: Who says I'm joking? HE LOOKS AT HER INCREDULOUSLY.

GRIFF: You're not serious? You are serious aren't you?

RUBY: Kevin used to be married. Wife not up to much - from what I can gather. I don't know what her job is. I take it it's to do with the military though because I heard Kevin say something about her being R.A.F.

GRIFF: Where's all this leading to?

RUBY: Well they had a little girl together. Now the ex-wife have picked up with yet another fella and he hasn't taken to her, poor little thing. There's a lot of talk of the little girl coming to live with Kevin.

GRIFF: In Nigel's house?

RUBY: Well where else?

GRIFF: SLIGHT PAUSE. If I don't take in all that's happening, you'll have to appreciate it's because things are moving a bit too fast for me.

RUBY: Too fast?

GRIFF: Last week I thought I had an average twenty five year old son who lived alone and had a mortgage in Pontypridd. Today he's a drag queen who shares a house and bed with a man who's already been married and who's daughter is about to move in. I mean there's only so much a guard with British Rail can grasp.

RUBY: Oh I don't know, I think you've grasp it all pretty well, Griff.

GRIFF: Will you tell me what the hell's happening to us?

RUBY: Keep your voice down - you're in a hospital remember.

GRIFF: I don't care where I am! Up till last Saturday our family was quite..... HE SEARCHES FOR THE WORD. Orthodox.

RUBY: Ortho? orthodox? Christ Griff, you can call us a lot of things but we've hardly been that.

GRIFF: On the surface we were. Now all of a sudden everything's a mess.

RUBY: No it's not.

GRIFF: SHOUTING. If people make fun of our son, it's a mess! If you get talked about by women in cars, it's a mess! If my work mates take the piss, believe, it's a bloody mess!

RUBY: You shouldn't care what people say.

GRIFF: But I do! It matters when they crack a joke and I can't laugh because we're the butt of it.

RUBY: I don't suppose we get a fraction of the flack Nigel does. If he can take the slings and arrows, why can't we? If we stick together as a family, Griff no-one can hurt us.

GRIFF: You don't know what it's like for me. What it was like for me on Saturday night.

RUBY: All right I'll admit, finding out the way you did that Nigel was a drag artist perhaps came as a bit of a shock to you but you've just got to come to terms with it just like I did.

GRIFF: It's not as easy for me.

RUBY: I wish you wouldn't keep saying "It's not easy for you".

GRIFF: INSISTING. It's not!

RUBY: Well it should be.

GRIFF: Why?

RUBY: Well.... I mean, you're normal enough now...

GRIFF: What do you mean?

RUBY: When we were courting I used to wonder which side of the fence you were going to fall.

GRIFF: You're all right, are you?

RUBY: Everybody has a mate, you know I understand that... but you couldn't move without that Richie Thomas. Talk about Tweedle Dumb and Tweedle Dee? He was like your shadow till I put my foot down.

GRIFF: There was nothing funny about me and Richie. We were like brothers we were.

RUBY: You don't take your brother with you on honeymoon.

GRIFF: SHOUTING. I didn't take him on honeymoon.

RUBY: SHOUTING BACK. It's hell of a coincidence then that he ended up in the caravan next to us, don't you think?

GRIFF: It's not fair to throw Richie up. Specially now he's not here to defend himself.

RUBY: I'd have said exactly the same thing if he was alive.

GRIFF: You're a dangerous woman, you are, Ruby.

RUBY: I put it all behind me and didn't think much more about it.... but after you made a fool of yourself at his funeral it brought it all back.

GRIFF: How many times have I got to tell you... there was never anything like that between us.

RUBY: Funny how he never got married.

GRIFF: You want to know why he didn't get married.

RUBY: Go on, surprise me.

GRIFF: I will. SLIGHT PAUSE. He loved somebody who was already married and it wasn't me... it was you. SLIGHT PAUSE. Well, what do you say to that?

RUBY: I knew. SLIGHT PAUSES Now what do you say?

GRIFF IS SPEECHLESS. A SLIGHT PAUSE BEFORE THE NURSE COMES OUT OF NIGEL'S ROOM.

NURSE: There we are then, he's all done and sitting up in bed waiting for you.

THE NURSE MAKES TO GO.

GRIFF: Er, Nurse....

THE NURSE TURNS AROUND.

GRIFF: Just now.... um.... HE FINDS IT HARD TO APOLOGISE. What it was.... Um....

NURSE: It's all right - forget it.

RUBY: No! It's not all right, is it, Griff?

GRIFF: I shouldn't have.... you know - shouted er, like that. You all do a good job.... deserve better....

RUBY: He's apologising but it doesn't come easy as you can see.

GRIFF: Does he know I'm here?

NURSE: He asked again. I lied.

GRIFF: Thank you.

NURSE: I didn't lie for you I lied for him. NODDING TOWARDS NIGEL'S ROOM. SLIGHT PAUSE. It's no big deal, you know. You can change your mind and go in if you want to. SLIGHT PAUSE. Anyway, I've got to go. HE SMILES AND LEAVES.

RUBY: He's a nice fella, isn't he? MEANING THE NURSE. Reminds me of Richie Thomas. SLIGHT PAUSE. He came to the house in a hell of a state one day. HE LOOKS AT HER. Richie. He told me how he felt about me ... then I told him how he felt about you and the poor bugger went home in a worse state than when he came in. SLIGHT PAUSE. I don't believe for a minute you ever got involved, but.... you can't deny you didn't know how he felt about you.

GRIFF: We grew up together.

RUBY: All right so as far as you were concerned you were close. He had feelings for you -

GRIFF: And you -

RUBY: That he shouldn't have had and you knew it. You accepted it and understood it. Why can't you show something of the same for your son.

GRIFF: It's different when it's your own. And anyway, Richie never dressed up in women's clothes, or wanted to as far as I know.

RUBY: Good God Griff it's only a bit of fun you've said that yourself.

GRIFF: I can take a joke and have a laugh as good as the next man - but you've got to admit what our Nigel's into is a hell of a lot deeper than that.

RUBY: All right so he does take it a bit more serious. He's got to. It's his job. There's nothing more to it than that. At the end of the day all the dresses get put away in a wardrobe.

GRIFF: Who said?

RUBY: Hell's delight, do you think he walks around the house in a dress do you?

GRIFF: It's possible. Who's to say he isn't sitting in there now waiting for us dressed up in a sisters' uniform.

RUBY: LAUGHING. Good, you're making a joke of it.

GRIFF: I'm dead bloody serious.

RUBY: SLIGHT PAUSE. Would it be so awful if he was? HE DOESN'T ANSWER. It shouldn't matter to us if he wanted to go around naked with a frying pan on his head.

GRIFF: You can say all you want, I can't like him for what he does.

RUBY: All right don't... you can still love him for what he is.

GRIFF: You mean in spite of what he is.

RUBY: Whatever. No-body really cares what he does behind his front door, Griff and if they do, why should it matter to us?

GRIFF: You're very good at all this aren't you. Much better than me.

RUBY: I've had more time. It'll get easier if you try, I promise.

GRIFF: But it'll never go away.

RUBY: No, Griff... it'll never go away - you can be sure of that. SLIGHT PAUSE. Can I ask you something? HE LOOKS AT HER. Which was the worst for you? The humiliation on Saturday night, or the knowledge that your only son is gay.

GRIFF: SHOUTING. It's not fair!

RUBY: Of course it's not, but life never is. SLIGHT PAUSE. I want to know what the hardest thing is for you. See, if it's the fact that he's gay, well there's nothing anybody including Nigel can do about that. If on the other hand it's the drag thing asking Nigel to give up the dresses isn't going to change him either.

GRIFF: Do you know what I've gone and done?

RUBY: Surprise me.

GRIFF: You know you brought Nigel's suitcases home with you after the accident? The suitcases with all the costumes? SLIGHT PAUSE. I've emptied them. I emptied them into two big plastic bags and put them out with the rubbish bin this morning.

RUBY: SLIGHT PAUSE. Oh my god, you thought that would solve everything and that would be the end of it, I suppose?

GRIFF: I don't know what I thought. SLIGHT PAUSE. After Saturday maybe I just wanted to get my own back.

RUBY: There was over five hundred pounds worth of dresses in those cases. Not to mention the make-up and wigs.

GRIFF: What can I say?

RUBY: Well nothing to me. I'd start thinking about how you're going to tell Nigel if I were you.

GRIFF: I don't know if I can apologise to him.

RUBY: And you won't know unless you try. Anyway, seems to me there's apologies due on both sides. See him - go on. Go in and -

GRIFF: You don't know what you're asking. *more*

RUBY: I'm only asking the same of you as I ask of myself. SLIGHT PAUSE. And you still haven't answered my question.

GRIFF: SLIGHT PAUSE. Going round the clubs like he does.. it's a bit like having a tattoo on his forehead.

RUBY: So it's not that he's gay then - it's the drag factor?

GRIFF: Why has everybody got to know?

RUBY: You'd feel better if he tried to hide it?

GRIFF: I'd feel better if he didn't flaunt it.

RUBY: So it is the drag factor.

GRIFF: I'm never going to be able to accept it like you.

RUBY: There's only one way to accept it, Griff and that's a little bit at a time. The first hurdle is to walk in through that door - the second is to smile, and if he smiles back, which he will..... everything will be plain sailing after that.

GRIFF: How can I smile when I feel like knocking seven different colours of shit out of him?

RUBY: You'll smile, Griff. We both will because the chips are down and we can't do anything else. SLIGHT PAUSE. When he was a little boy, all I wished was for him to be happy.... and he is. I forgot to wish for me to be happy too.

GRIFF: We can always walk away - let him get on with it.

RUBY: SHRUGS. I can't do that, he's my son - he needs me.

GRIFF: Oh well there you are then..... as long as he's got you -

RUBY: And I need him. And although it's not easy for you to admit, you need him too.

GRIFF: Does he need me, do you think? *cross*

RUBY: The answer to that is staring you in the face, Griff. It wasn't me he asked the nurse about. It was you.

GRIFF: He only wants me to condone what he's doing.

RUBY: He's not after your blessing. He needs you to accept him for what he is, that's not the same thing.

GRIFF: What about what I need?

RUBY: Shouldn't come into it. Roots and wings, Griff... roots and wings. SLIGHT PAUSE. You can walk away now if you want to but it's not going to solve anything. SLIGHT PAUSE. Whether you like it or not, you're going to be his father for an awful long time. SLIGHT PAUSE. Closing your eyes is not going to make him disappear. SLIGHT PAUSE.I'm going in - I bet he's wondering what's happening. SHE MAKES AT NIGEL'S DOOR.

GRIFF: Do you want me to come with you?

RUBY: Of course I do... but there's no way I'll let you. Not with me. You go in there, you go in on your own. SLIGHT PAUSE. Well what's it to be, Griff? Is it time to take your head out of the sand or what? SLIGHT PAUSE. Come on, it can't be as bad as all that. One small step for Griff, one giant leap for Nigel. SLIGHT PAUSE.. If it makes you feel any better you'll be killing two birds with one stone. HE LOOKS AT HER. You remember that weight we talked about? You know, the one Nigel took off his chest and put on mine? You can't take it away, I know that..... but I'd sleep a hell of a lot easier if you took half. Isn't that what husbands are for?

GRIFF: And sons?

RUBY: SLIGHT PAUSE. Kids. They're all the same when it comes down to it.... arm ache when they're small - heart ache when grown.

THEY SHARE A MOMENT BEFORE SHE TURNS AND GOES INTO NIGEL'S ROOM.

RUBY: OFF. Hiya luv, you're looking marvellous.

GRIFF STANDS MOTIONLESS FOR A MOMENT. SLOWLY HE TURNS TO LOOK INTO NIGEL'S ROOM. AFTER STARING IN FOR A MOMENT OR TWO HE MOVES AWAY TO THE CHAIRS WHERE HE HAS LEFT HIS WORK BAG. HE PICKS IT UP AND SLOWLY WALKS TO THE DOOR AGAIN. AFTER A BRIEF PAUSE HE OPENS THE DOOR AND STANDS JUST INSIDE.

the end

Frank Vickery had his first play performed in 1977. Since then he has written extensively for television, radio and the theatre. Almost all his stage plays are published by SAMUEL FRENCH Ltd of London. For television, Frank has written episodes of "THE DISTRICT NURSE", "WALES PLAYHOUSE" and more recently, "LIFEBOAT" - all for the BBC. "THE NECKTIE PARTY" and "KILLING TIME" are just two of the series Frank has written for BBC Radio and he has just put the finishing touches to his very own sitcom, based on his stage play "FAMILY PLANNING", for S4C.

Simply set in a hospital corridor, "THE DRAG FACTOR" is classic Frank Vickery. It is a poignant and blisteringly funny account of a husband and wife coming abruptly to terms with the fact that their son is gay. Certain to be a festival favourite, the characters of RUBY and GRIFF offer brilliant opportunities for middle- aged actors. The small role of the male nurse completes the cast.

The Drama Association of Wales
exists to provide opportunities for people to be creatively involved in drama which is fun and of a high standard. The Association runs the world's largest drama hire service and sends scripts and theatre books to members worldwide. As well as the library service, the Drama Association runs training courses and festivals and provides many other services for drama lovers. As a key function, the Association stimulates and publishes new playwriting.

ISBN 1-8987400-7-0

The Sinus Handbook

A Self-Help Guide

Muriel MacFarlane, R.N., M.A.